lift off

lift off
100 tips to energize

Sarah Merson

MQP

Published by **MQ Publications Limited**
12 The Ivories, 6–8 Northampton Street
London N1 2HY
Tel: +44 (0) 20 7359 2244
Fax:+44 (0) 20 7359 1616
email: mail@mqpublications.com
website: www.mqpublications.com

Copyright © MQ Publications Limited 2003

TEXT: **Copyright © 2003 Sarah Merson**
DESIGN: **Balley Design Associates**
SERIES EDITOR: **Yvonne Deutch**

ISBN: 1-84072-520-6

10 9 8 7 6 5 4 3 2 1

Printed and bound in China

contents

introduction

Energy! You just can't seem to get enough of it. In fact, you may find it hard going just to get through the day. Often, it's not physically demanding activity that tires you out—it's more likely that you're exhausted by the stress of a busy, multitasking lifestyle. This includes the triumphs and disasters of daily business, pressured deadlines, heavy workloads, the complexity of organizing family and personal relationships, plus a hectic social life.

Modern living requires a massive amount of energy, so much so that you may find that your "get up and go" has got up and gone. Indeed, research shows that conditions such as chronic fatigue syndrome are on the increase, and that many people are suffering from varying degrees of lethargy, or exhaustion.

If you've lost your energetic spark, here's the solution. *LIFT OFF* offers 100 ingenious tips to energize yourself, and to maintain your energy levels. So, dive right in and check out the various ways to get yourself full of enthusiasm for life once more. Whether you try bouncing on a trampoline, drinking a reviving tea, or transforming your mental and emotional attitudes, *LIFT OFF* shows you how to get the extra energy to cope with your life, and how to go about your day with zip, zest, and vitality.

CHAPTER ONE

food for lift off

1 Juice it up

Brightly colored fruit and vegetables are packed with plant nutrients that ignite energy and enhance your health. And one way of enjoying these benefits is by extracting their delicious, rejuvenating juices. The choice is dazzling: apple, pear, mango, strawberry, carrot, celery, spinach, and beetroot juices all carry the potent living energy of highly concentrated vitamins, minerals, and enzymes—everything you need to live life to the full. So, go on! capture the dynamic power of juices by investing in a juicer and squeeze the life out of your favorite fruit and vegetables.

2 Raw energy

Unlock the pure energy of raw, organic seasonal foods, and give yourself a treat at the same time. In their uncooked, unadulterated state, fruit, nuts, seeds, salads, sea vegetables, and herbs provide you with maximum amounts of extractable energy and the highest levels of vitamins and minerals. Whenever possible, eat these foods raw to avoid losing nutrients during cooking. Choose organic products because they are untainted by chemicals, and eat seasonal foods that haven't been subjected to artificial growth hormones. You'll enjoy the finest flavors and optimum health benefits.

3 Kick start your day

Instead of relying on the caffeine hit that comes with your morning cup of coffee, try one of nature's great energy-boosters, the Brazilian herb guarana. A 500mg capsule contains just 15mg of caffeine, compared with the 80–120mg that you get in a cup of coffee. You'll also get the added benefit of special compounds in guarana that slow down the assimilation of caffeine. So, if you're addicted to coffee, wean yourself off that java jag and opt for guarana's sustained natural energy.

4 Delicious detox

Detox often conjures up images of self-denial and suffering, but it needn't be hell. Make it a positive pleasure by incorporating delicious foods into your detox menu. Try kiwi fruit (rich in Vitamin C), dark leafy greens (full of zinc), garlic, and wholesome, energizing dishes such as hearty root vegetable soups and casseroles, pasta, and baked potatoes. A well-planned program clears your system of toxins, boosts your immune system, fights off vitality draining infections such as colds and flu, and restores your zest for life.

5 Are you green?

Known as nature's finest medicine, wheatgrass is a complete food that contains all known nutrients. Many alternative practitioners recommend it for blood purification, liver detoxification, and system cleansing, all of which utilize its powerful energizing properties. It also contains chlorophyll, which is capable of absorbing energy directly from the sun. So, if you've never tried it before, why not harness the rejuvenating powers of wheatgrass by getting some the next time you're at your local health food store? Whether you drink it as a juice, take it in the powder form, or take it as a supplement, you'll reap its great benefits.

6 Va va voom !

Want to know how to get
a secret source of energy
to get you up and running?
Just go back to nature and get
some herbs! Nettles are tops! They're
highly nutritious and packed with zinc, iron,
and B vitamins. Wash the young tips of the
plants, and steam them to eat as a
vegetable, or make them into a tea or
broth. Nettles actively restore energy by
stimulating your adrenal glands—when
these are exhausted, they are major
energy depletors.

- Lemon balm is a wonderful
  remedy for lifting the
  spirits and has a long

tradition of banishing melancholy and depression.

- Milk Thistle stimulates and cleanses the system. It clears toxicity, dispels stagnation and sluggishness, and boosts energy.

7 Eat breakfast

It's tempting to skip food and grab a quick cup of coffee in the morning, but energy-wise, it's a big mistake. If you miss breakfast, you're liable to suffer from depressed mental energy, poor memory, and lack of concentration. When you wake up, your blood sugar levels are low, and you need to restore them to give you energy for the day. What you eat is important too—choose carbohydrates such as whole grains and porridge oats, which release energy slowly and steadily, rather than refined foods such as white bread or sugary cereals. This will ensure that your body and brain are supplied with consistent levels of glucose for glowing mental and physical performance.

8 Sweet nothings

How many times have you reached for something sweet when you need a quick pick-me-up? Sure, you'll get an instant boost, but you'll be dumped back down in no time at all. Sugary snacks contain high levels of glucose or sucrose, which is rapidly absorbed into the bloodstream. The pancreas responds to this by producing far too much insulin (a hormone which breaks down sugar). This leads to a rapid drop in sugar levels, which leaves you feeling even more exhausted than before. Watch out for alcohol and caffeine, too—they have similar effects.

9 Bubbling over

Can you remember your last glass of champagne? And, can you remember how bubbly you felt afterwards? Champagne bottles are corked after the first fermentation. This, in turn, causes the second fermentation to produce a great deal of carbon dioxide. Then, as it builds up, this creates the bubbles that make champagne so special. The process also creates tyramine, a substance that releases stimulating hormones. These excite your peripheral muscles and intensify the beating of your heart, bringing a feeling of exhilaration to your whole system. So, for special lift off occasions, crack open the lovely bubbly!

10 Crucial fuel

Carbohydrates are like jet fuel for the body. Without them, and the glycogen they produce, you're bound to feel tired. They keep blood sugar levels steady and help muscles to get more fuel to keep you bright and active. For reliable energy, choose slow-releasing carbohydrate foods such as pasta, porridge oats, wholemeal bread, and baked potatoes. Protein is another valuable food that is essential for energy; but, remember, it's not just found in meat. You can also get plenty from fish and a range of vegetables such as soy beans and chick peas!

11 A great tonic

After uninterrupted use in China for over 2,000 years, Siberian Ginseng is now popular all over the world. Use it to restore immediate and long-term energy, and to overcome stress and fatigue. It works by increasing the supply of oxygen to all the cells in your body, thereby improving your endurance and alertness. It also helps to maintain your blood sugar levels. Ginseng is widely available in capsule form. But, if you prefer, you can easily make yourself a cup of invigorating ginseng tea. Add one teaspoon of the dried root (available at health stores and Asian food stores) to one cup of water, bring to a boil, and simmer for ten minutes.

12 Get passionate about food

On your next visit to the supermarket, instead of walking around on autopilot, stop to look and think about the foods on display and choose those that really appeal to your senses. Maybe you like the color, the shape, the texture, or smell of a certain food? Wherever possible, choose something that you've never tried before, and enjoy preparing it as a creative adventure. This new excitement and energy will be passed on to the food in the eating and will have you bounding back to the store for more.

13 Drink tea

Several tea blends have amazing energizing powers. Green tea is especially effective, due to its decongestant, anti-inflammatory, and refreshing properties, and its ability to aid absorption of vitamins that boost immunity. Oolong tea is another good choice; it's a great digestive aid, an effective stimulant, and gives a positive mood boost. Then there's red tea; it brightens you up, is low in caffeine, and is also strongly digestive. Alternatively, you may prefer the flavorsome lift from a herbal tea.

21

14 Salad days

Make your daily salads into something special—glorious arrangements of life-giving, fresh ingredients. We're talking gorgeous, crispy, mouth-watering greens here—curly endive, romaine, radicchio, and lamb's lettuce mixed with wild herbs such as basil, tarragon, coriander, and flat leaf parsley. Also, add some edible flowers such as marigold petals for their brilliant color.

15 Little and often

Food is the basic fuel that we all need to get energy; but, in order to keep this energy ongoing, it's important to refuel at regular intervals. Long periods between eating deplete the body of its glycogen reserves and, as a result, energy levels dip. To avoid this, try eating small snacks throughout the day. Don't allow yourself to get hungry at any one time, and when you do eat, don't pig out on a huge meal, as that will make you feel sluggish.

16 Know your ying from your yang

Take the Chinese approach, and eat foods that balance the effect of the changing season on your body. In Chinese terms, some foods are yin, whereas others are yang. Concentrate on yin foods such as bananas, crab, duck, lettuce, tofu, grapefruit, and watermelon in the summer, and yang foods such as chicken, lamb, prawns, peaches, raspberries, walnuts, and sunflower seeds in winter. This will keep you properly energized all year round.

17 Take five

In addition to being low in fat and high in fiber, fresh fruit and vegetables provide you with a range of nutrients that keep your whole system in good order and stave off constipation and other digestive problems that zap your energy levels. They're also rich in powerful antioxidants, which fight infection. So, make it your aim to eat at least five portions of fruit and vegetables each day.

18 Water your body

Energize yourself by drinking at least eight to ten 8oz glasses of water every day. About 55-60 percent of your body is composed of water, most of it residing in your cells, where it enables essential tasks such as the breakdown of carbohydrates for brain fuel. In fact, your brain is more than 70 percent water by weight, and if this level dips below a critical point, you'll soon feel listless and dull. Water is drained from your system by dry, indoor air, exercise, and high-caffeine drinks. So, for optimal brain and body function, make sure you drink plenty of water at regular intervals throughout the day.

19 Discover friendly fats

Many of us have a threatening image of fat as an implicitly bad food, but that depends on what kind of fat we're talking about. It's true that trans-fatty acids (found in foods such as butter) slow down your energy. But essential fatty acids (found in avocados, sesame seeds, and oily fish such as salmon and mackerel) actually improve your energy levels, brain cell communication, stamina, and endurance. So, before jumping to conclusions, it's worth a trip to the library, or a browse on the internet, so you can wise up on what's really best for you in the food you eat.

20 Gut reaction

If you're constantly tired, you may have a food intolerance. Recent estimates indicate that about 45 percent of the population may have this problem, with peanuts, shellfish, dairy products, wheat, and gluten as the most common offenders. This suggests that nearly half of us could be walking around with related symptoms, one of which is unusually low energy. If you suspect that you have a problem with a particular food, try avoiding it for a while. Provided you've identified the correct food, this should relieve the symptoms and give your body a rest. Then watch your energy levels take a leap in the right direction.

27

fit for lift off

21 Bounce, bounce, bounce

Jump on a trampoline if you really want to let yourself go. As you bound through the air with reckless abandonment, gaining more and more height with each bounce, a flood of exhilaration and energy fills your body. You're used to walking on the earth, with the ground under your feet to steady and confine you. But once you get airborne, with your feet and your hair flying, the adrenaline will rush through your system and energize you beyond imagination. Watch out, though, this is an addictive form of energy, which will get you bouncing crazy.

22 Qigong stretch

Qigong is an exercise method that is rapidly becoming popular in the West. "Qi" means energy and "gong" means practice. Qigong has been used in the East for thousands of years to activate "qi," and has a significant effect on clearing stress, removing tension, aiding relaxation, and promoting energy. Try this simple qigong stretch: move your hands upward and outward in front of your body so that your palms are held high above your head and face upward. Look up and keep your back straight. Perform the stretch in a slow and relaxed way.

23 Replenish energy

At those moments when you are utterly exhausted, try this. Lie on your back with your legs outstretched and your arms by your sides. Position your arms slightly away from your body and keep your legs slightly apart. Turn your palms upward and close your eyes. Focus on your breathing—with each breath out, release all the tension in your muscles. Doing this simple exercise for just ten minutes lowers your blood pressure and is said to give you the energy equivalent to a night's sleep.

24 Just dance!

Dancing is a fabulous, fun way of toning your entire body and putting the color back into your cheeks, especially when it's something exotic and rhythmic, like salsa classes. Your fitness levels soar and will naturally boost your energy. The vigorous movement will make you feel gloriously liberated, and you'll get a wonderful buzz from the music. Dancing brings you a happy psychological high that is hard to beat. And, remember, when you choose salsa or other dance forms that include a partner, you'll also have the added benefits of being motivated by others and their energetic vibes.

25 Get moving

You may think you're just too shattered to exercise, but if you want to regain that extra edge on life, then daily exercise is the way to go. The more physically fit and active you are, the more energy you can store and produce at short notice. The key to success is not how hard you exercise, but how often. If you can't manage the gym or classes, then get a home fitness video. Alternatively, take two 15-minute walks every day. Exercise not only gets you fit, it releases natural endorphins into your system, which will get you feeling happier.

26 Sleep well

Exercise induces a sound and restful sleep, which gives you plenty of get up and go for the next day. In fact, to keep your energy levels at their peak, you need to get a good night's sleep every night. To achieve this goal make sure you do some exercise each day, as well as devising a restful bedtime routine. This may involve taking a warm bath with a few drops of essential oil of lavender, sipping a cup of camomile tea, and ensuring that your bedroom is quiet, dark, and cool—perfect for sleeping.

27 Don't overdo it

You can overstrain or overexert yourself with exercise; if you do, this will lead to tension and added stress, and will deplete, rather than enhance, your energy levels. When you push your body beyond its limits, you may pay the price with an impaired immune system. This is because exercise produces a chemical called glutamine, which stimulates immunity. After overexertion, glutamine levels plummet, leaving you more open to infection. It will also put stress on your adrenals. So, exercise by all means, but learn your limits.

28 Progressive relax

Relaxation exercises like this are important energy providers:

- Lie flat on your back with arms and legs outstretched.
- Take your attention from the top of your head, over your face, neck, chest, abdomen, thighs, knees, legs, ankles, and toes, relaxing every fiber as you go.
- Then focus on the back of your head, neck, back, waist, thighs, right down to your feet.
- Finally, focus on the outer sides of your head, neck, shoulders, upper arms, elbows, right down to your feet.
- Repeat as many times as you wish, until you're totally relaxed.

29 Serene power

Quiet forms of exercise such as yoga and T'ai chi have unique health benefits. T'ai chi boosts immunity and overall well-being, and allows energy to flow through the body unhindered. As for yoga, it has positive effects on pulse rates, blood pressure, and mental and physical performance. Together, these ancient systems promote fine equilibrium and lasting vitality.

30 Meridian lift

This subtle Chinese exercise boosts energy to the brain. Take a deep breath in and out. Let your mind go blank. Rest your hand lightly over your pubic bone, and trace your hand slowly upward until it reaches your bottom lip. Bring your hand to the side, away from your body, then bring it back to rest just above your pubic bone. Repeat twice more.

31 Magnetic energy

During exercise, blood and lymph flow freely and become an internal source of the magnetic energy on which you thrive. In particular, aerobic exercise causes your heart to beat firmly and your breathing to deepen. This heightens fluid movement and connects you with your own power, as it intensifies the electromagnetic field on which your body and mind run. When you take in extra oxygen, you're revitalized to the core—right through to your cells. Exercise also helps mobilize and eliminate toxins, which are serious energy drainers.

32 Jumping Jacks

If you want to have fun and get yourself in the mood for energetic action, try a session of Jumping Jacks. Start from a standing position with feet together, arms by your sides, and knees slightly bent. Then, in one fluid motion, pull yourself up by swinging your arms sideways, while opening your legs about a shoulder width apart. Touch your hands above your head with arms straight. Bring your feet back together and hands to your sides. Ta da! That's a Jumping Jack. Aim to do them for 2 minutes a day, and you'll be rewarded with a huge surge of energy.

33 Running on high

It's no coincidence that experienced athletes describe a feeling of euphoria, or a "runner's high," which gives them the ultimate motivation to make it to the finish line. When the body is exhausted, it produces endorphins and morphine-like substances that act as natural painkillers. These same chemicals are released when you experience pleasure, and bring inspiration and momentum with them. You don't have to compete in a marathon to experience this sense of exhilaration—it can be gained from a vigorous run, a workout at the gym, or an aerobics class.

34 Skip around

Remember how you felt as a child, running, skipping, and jumping around in the summer sun? Chances are you haven't felt that alive throughout your adult life. Although you may not have had a care in the world back then, all that mischievous, energetic play sent you into a state of beaming liveliness, and you literally jumped for joy. Since then, you've probably put inhibiting constraints on yourself and your unique expression of vitality. So, if you want to revive that ultimate energy of mind, body, and soul, get yourself a skipping rope, and enjoy jumping and running around as if you were five years old again.

43

35 Good morning!

Start the morning with this invigorating warm up routine:

- Stand with your feet shoulder-width apart and place your hands just beneath your navel. Breathe into your belly, filling your abdomen, and as you breathe out, pull your abdomen in.
- Rub your hands together and rotate your wrists.
- Rub your face and tap your head, neck, and shoulders firmly.
- Lift your shoulders and rotate them backward and forward.
- Allow your arms to swing freely from side to side. Keep your legs strong and the top part of your body loose.

36 Take a hike

If you automatically associate exercise with trips to the gym, you may want to hide under the covers at the very thought. But there is a more scenic option. Hiking in the countryside will give you all the benefits of exercise, and also offers you spectacular

44

views and tranquil, natural settings. Once you get into it, you'll feel a real sense of achievement at the ground you've covered, the sights you've seen, the fresh air you've breathed, and the vitality you feel. So, make exercise a pleasure, not a pain.

37 Zest for life

Is your hair dull and lifeless? And are your nails brittle and prone to breaking easily? Lack of exercise can result in calcium and magnesium being leached from your bones, hair, and nails, and this will leave them in a weakened state. Taking nutritional supplements is the couch potato remedy for this, but there's really nothing like exercise to transform your core health. It plays a key part in the constant renewal process of cells in your body and offers, among countless rewards, a deep, glowing radiance. Someone who is physically active comes across as powerful, full of vital energy, and infused with an irresistible zest for life.

38 Have fun

If you think you should exercise, but hate every minute, then you're putting yourself under more stress than it's worth. Sure, when you begin, you may not have total enthusiasm; but once you establish consistency, you'll feel energized to do more. To find an exercise that gets you leaping out of bed on a Sunday morning, pick the one that makes you feel good about yourself and is fun enough to put a smile on your face.

39 Funky and flexible

Bored with your regular aerobics class? Then think about going to a jazzercise or salsarobics session instead. These funky classes offer a combination of choreographed jazz, or tantalizing salsa, complete with an energetic aerobic workout—you'll do a thorough warm up and stretch before getting down to the beat. The focus is on learning single dance steps first, before adding them together to form a longer sequence. The benefits are enormous; you'll feel more toned and flexible, and, motivated by the music, you'll be ablaze with vitality.

40 Take a dip

Can you recall the times when you sat on the edge of the pool, psyching yourself up to take the plunge? When you finally did it, and your body hit the water, it was as if an electric shock of euphoria passed through you; and, as you swam through the water, remember how liberated and free you felt. Wasn't that a great feeling? Next time you're in need of an electric zap of vitality and thrilling energy, maybe you should take a dip. Don't limit yourself to your local pool, though—why not brave the ocean or a river? You'll be amazed at how good you feel.

CHAPTER THREE

mind lift off

41 Deep waters

When you take a deep, calm look within yourself, your innate energy moves effortlessly and empowers you to do anything you choose. The more that energy is obstructed, however, the slower it flows. You need to learn how to harness the power of your personal energy, by allowing it to move freely and without restraint. You can do this through meditation. With regular meditation, you become more able to focus on the task at hand, instead of dissipating your energy by trying to do many things at the same time. That's why people who practice meditation on a regular basis have been shown to have higher and sustained energy levels.

42 Breath of life

Breathing is the key to your survival; it provides oxygen for your body to generate energy to move, think, and feel. Yet, experts say that most of us use less than one third of our lung capacity. So, if you want to get sufficient oxygen to feel fully energized, it's a good idea to practice healthy breathing. Sit comfortably and focus on your breath. Breathe deeply and fully, allowing your belly to expand as you inhale. Know that, as you breathe in, you are taking in new life and energy, and as you breathe out, concentrate on spreading that energy around your body.

43 Take control

Experts agree that it is a loss of control over your life that drains energy levels. This could relate to any number of lifestyle habits (e.g., eating, drinking, smoking, and working to excess) or could be connected to issues such as financial insecurity, or emotional hang-ups. Making even the smallest of changes can bring transformation; once you've regained a bit of personal control, yours is the power again, and with power comes revived energy and vigor for life. So, whatever holds you back, take that first step now; control of your own destiny is paramount.

44 Change the picture

A change really is as good as a rest. It's easy to get tunnel vision and become preoccupied in your daily tasks. Just as soon as you break the cycle, however, and do something different, or even in a different order, you can get a whole new perspective on life and regain an energetic spirit. It may simply mean taking an alternative route to work, or going to bed with a book on a weekend, rather than watching the usual late night film. Whatever change you choose, that shift in thinking will add an uplifting spring to your step.

45 Look at yourself

Visualization is a powerful tool. You can use it to feel full of energy. Get yourself into a deeply relaxed state and see yourself jumping out of bed every morning at 7 A.M., to go for a run, to swim energetically, or to go to the gym in the evening. As you focus on the image, watch yourself radiating energy and well-being. How do you look? How do you feel? Wouldn't you like to experience that every minute of every day? Well, you can. Visualization not only helps you to see yourself differently, it will motivate and energize you to turn your images into reality.

46 Good for you

Pleasure is hugely important, as it keeps your mind vibrating on a positive frequency. The sources of joy in your life can be quite simple—think how much you enjoy getting involved in your favorite TV program, playing with your pets, eating the food you love, listening to a beautiful piece of music, and experiencing the bliss of good relationships. Also, don't underestimate the power of healthy living—a balanced diet, regular exercise, and fresh, clean air. This will help produce a stream of feel-good hormones in your brain and take you through each day, live and kicking.

47 Light fantastic

Leap out of bed with light therapy. Research shows that we're likely to feel mentally tired and lethargic when we're in darkness. Light stimulates the production of the feel-good hormone serotonin, and when it hits the pineal gland in the brain, it lowers levels of the sleep-inducing hormone melatonin. By using a light box, or waking up to a specially designed lamp that lights up gradually, your system will get going before you do, and by the time your alarm goes off, feelings of grogginess and lethargy will be replaced with boundless energy and enthusiasm.

48 Mind supplements

Try these natural memory and mind-boosters:

- Gingko Biloba is famous for enhancing mood and memory and improving concentration and energy by stimulating circulation of blood in the brain.
- Well known for it's anti-depressant properties, St. John's Wort can be used for the ultimate mental boost.
- Glutamine, an amino acid, can be used directly as fuel for the brain and has been shown to enhance mental alertness.
- Elevate your mood with an Omega 3 fish oil supplement.

49 Multi-colored mood

Have you ever noticed how different you feel when wearing a yellow shirt or when walking into a red room? Color can have great effect on your mood; this is due to individual wavelengths, and the electrical energy your brain receives when a color is absorbed by the photoreceptors in the retina of your eye. Yellow, the color of learning, lifts the spirits as it increases the pulse rate, whereas orange encourages appetite and reduces fatigue. In many cultures, orange is coupled with red, for physical energy and vitality.

50 Don't sweat it

We need a certain amount of stress just to motivate us to go about our daily tasks, but when levels become too high (otherwise known as negative stress), we feel harassed, nervous, pressured, and ultimately lacking in energy. You can lessen the effects by learning to prioritize and by keeping everything in perspective. Is it really the end of the world if you don't get to lunch on time? Do you have to go to the dentist and pick up your dry cleaning before picking up the kids from school? Mostly, you don't. So conserve all that precious energy for yourself instead.

51 You can do it

Do you have a yearning to learn French, or run the marathon this year? What's to stop you doing all the things you want to do? Often, it's sheer lack of self confidence. Don't let your energy be destroyed by negative beliefs about yourself and your abilities. Instead, use affirmations to spur you on—empowering phrases that you repeat aloud to yourself, replacing limiting thoughts and feelings with positive beliefs and the inspired energy to really make things happen.

52 Activate your mind

It is widely understood that keeping mentally active and alert helps your mind remain energetic. But this is a bit more complicated than it seems. It's not simply a matter of completing the daily crossword, or doing calculations in your head, instead of relying on a calculator. These are all functions of the logical, left side of your brain, and you use this part quite a lot. It's just as important to stimulate the right side, which is the creative and emotional center. Activities such as doodling, sketching, and humming, all give the left side a rest and set up a good flow of inspirational energy from one side of your brain to the other.

53 Brain massage

When you're mentally exhausted, it can be a great relief to rub the top of your head with your fingertips. In doing so, you're following an ancient tradition. Chinese head massage uses techniques that help *chi* energy to flow freely and create balance throughout the body. The treatment often begins with thumb and finger techniques, similar to acupressure, on the top of the head, and may include firm, pushing strokes and light, brisk invigorating movements. This releases stress from the brain area, awakens your mind, and energizes you throughout.

54 Be an optimist

Adopt a positive outlook—this, in itself, generates energy. Research has shown that people who see the glass as half empty are more likely to feel tired than those who see it as half full. This is because pessimism is far more energy-draining than optimism; the power of the mind is such that optimism breeds more energy, and energy produces even more optimism. So, when you next feel negativity creeping into your thoughts, try turning it around, and notice how your energy levels turn with it.

55 Watch the baby

When you spend time with children, you'll notice that they freely express themselves in the moment, whether they're happy, sad, angry, or tired. You'll also note that they always seem to have endless energy and zest for life. This is partly due to their innate ability to convey feelings spontaneously and openly. This applies to you, also. You don't have to behave like a baby; but when you allow your feelings to flow, unhindered by pressure to behave a certain way, your mind will feel unimpeded, and your natural energy will flow effortlessly and vivaciously.

56 Resist overload

Can you really work at full pitch from 8 A.M. to 7 P.M. every day, maintain close relationships, and run an active social life? Keeping all these balls in the air is all very well, and you may think you can manage it all; but expecting to retain a balanced flow of energy at the same time is a tall order. Chances are your mind will end up frazzled, and your performance will be compromised. In order to keep yourself mentally alert and energetic, it's a good idea to set boundaries. Be realistic about what you can and can't do.

57 What's your dosha?

Ayurvedic medicine classifies mind energy into three personality categories, or doshas.

Pitta Naturally sharp and quick minded, they love reading and doing mental puzzles, but too much intellectual work aggravates them. They need relaxing pastimes.

Kapha Slow thinkers, they generally benefit from extra mental stimulation, and should avoid boring, repetitive tasks.

Vata They dream up projects, and always have new schemes and ideas. They should avoid sensory stimulation and concentrate on one idea or task at a time.

58 Get ionized

The atmosphere contains both positive and negatively charged ions. An excess of positive ions can be exhausting, whereas negative ions boost your mental energy. Think of the charge that is released after a thunderstorm, when the air is dynamic and electrically charged with negative ions. Now think about how you felt then—probably more alert and uplifted. You don't have to wait until the next thunderstorm to get this buzz again—simply invest in a negative ion machine and transform your own atmosphere. You'll be mentally energized, come rain or shine.

59 Blue sky thinking

Confined or restrained in repetitive life patterns? Be careful—
your mental energy can easily become blocked. To prevent this,
experiment with ways to broaden your horizons and seek out
new inspiration. This may come from looking up to the sky on a
sunny day and actively imagining what lies beyond. It may even
come from talking to a stranger on the street, or taking a trip to
somewhere new. But, whatever you do, get out of that rut, look
around for new stimulation, and revel in the energy you
get from being open to what life offers.

60 Get passionate

When you become enthused by a visionary
life goal or ambition, messenger molecules
are released in your brain, and your mental
energy vibrates at a higher frequency. A variety
of signals are then sent from the brain around the
entire body, generating a flood of internal energy.
Some people are born with a clear mission or
purpose that urges them on. However, most of us
have to search for it. Never give up looking—always
go toward anything that inspires strong, even
passionate feelings in you, and spurs you into action.
The energy to achieve will come naturally.

emotional lift off

61 Bach flower remedies

These pure essences were developed early in the last century by Dr. Edward Bach, a physician and homeopath. After much research he concluded that illnesses are caused by negative mental states that affect physical health. He spent many years searching the countryside for a solution in the plant kingdom. Ultimately, he found 38 plants whose vibrations seemed to reharmonize negative mental states and work directly on emotional energy. With 38 to choose from, there's a remedy for everyone. Try the following:

Gentian an especially good remedy to use if you're feeling despondent or depressed

Olive works wonders for both mental and physical exhaustion

Clematis for when you're absent-minded, mentally dreamy

Mustard for depression without direct reason

Walnut the "link" breaker for times of change

Scleranthus for indecision, mood swings

Wild Rose for apathetic drifters, the unambitious

Wild Oat helps define goals

62 Set good goals

How can you stay motivated and energized when progress is
frustratingly slow? A lack of activity and direction can numb your
mind and emotions, and cause a rapid slump in energy levels.
One answer is to set yourself an achievable list of goals and
tasks, so you have something to focus on every day. Then, even
when a major pathway is blocked, you can still enjoy the
satisfaction of accomplishment. Better still, as each of your goals is
reached, you'll feel inspired to surmount the larger obstacles.

63 Paint a picture

If you're at an emotional dead end, you can release your blocked
energy by painting a picture. Get yourself some paints, a brush
and some paper, card, or canvas, and set your imagination free.
Even if you've never had an art lesson in your life, don't worry.
You're not aiming to paint a masterpiece. You're simply taking

yourself on an exploratory journey, enjoying the movement of the brush and the impact of the colors you use. You'll discover new sources of energy from your deepest creative centers.

64 Don't be scared

By trying to protect yourself from unwanted hurt, you may have become imprisoned by your own defenses. But this also blocks off positive feelings of trust and outgoing feeling. When this happens, use affirmation to knock down those barriers, and allow yourself to be vulnerable again. The theme can center around core statements such as "I can let myself trust," or "It's safe to express my feelings." Write down your chosen affirmation and think about its meaning. Try saying it to yourself 20 times each day—sometimes in front of a mirror, while looking yourself in the eye. Continue doing this until you begin to feel released from fear. Your emotions will run free again.

65 Scent trail

Next time you're passing a perfume counter, stop a while, and revitalize your emotions with sweet memories of the past or enticing visions of the future. Take yourself back into the arms of a lover by smelling a certain perfume or cologne; or allow your emotions to react to the experience of a new scent trail.

Perfumes carry powerful emotional charges—memories waiting to be unlocked or desires waiting to be fulfilled. Either way, let perfume work its evocative magic on you, and give yourself an amazing emotional high.

66 Turn up the music

Music is a great emotional stimulant—it may remind you of a time, a place, or a particular person. It can conjure up certain images or simply make you feel profoundly good about yourself. Wherever you are, whether it's in your car, your kitchen, or in the bath, and you need a wonderful emotional lift, play some of your favorite tunes, and play them loudly. Let the music seep into every corner of your body and soul. Your emotional energy is guaranteed to come out buzzing.

67 Emotional detox

Just as you need to cleanse your body with detox programs and herbal supplements, you also need to detox on an emotional level. Modern life takes its toll, but there are various techniques you can use to bring healthy emotional energy back into play. Try meditation, yoga, Qigong, or visualizations; or, alternatively, book yourself in with a counselor or therapist, who will assist and guide you in releasing tangled emotions. As a result, your emotional energy will switch on, and you'll soon be bouncing back into action.

68 Work up a sweat

You may not relish the thought of taking exercise, but you may like to know that a session at the gym can ignite your sexual energy. In one study, 25 percent of the women questioned had been sexually aroused during a workout. Research has also shown that men who go for regular workouts have a raised libido, better sex, and experience fewer erectile problems. The men who followed an aerobic fitness program four times a week for nine months had 30 percent more sex and 26 percent more orgasms than before. So, if you want a sure-fire way to pep up your sexual vigor, go work up a sweat.

69 Treat yourself

When was the last time you really indulged yourself? Maybe you'd love a day at a health farm, or a long vacation, or perhaps nothing would satisfy you more right now than a session of retail therapy. Whatever you wish for, make sure you indulge yourself from time to time. Relish the sense of freedom and adventure that comes when you throw caution to the wind, leaving behind your daily life, routine, and obligations for just one moment. Go on, treat yourself nicely, and feel your emotions soar.

70 Plan your time

To avoid downward plunges in emotional energy, don't cram too many things into your day. However much you imagine you can do, you can only fit a certain amount into the time available. When you try to do more, or even anticipate an impossible list of tasks to accomplish, you're setting yourself up for failure, and your emotional energy suffers accordingly. Instead, go for paced activities within your capabilities, while ensuring that you take time out for yourself. Result? You'll feel cool, balanced, and more energetic.

71 You sexy thing

The sheer power of thought can greatly increase your sexual energy. All you need do is visualize yourself as a glorious sex goddess or god. Think of a phrase such as "I'm so, so sexy!" and repeat it to yourself as you lie in bed, while imagining yourself initiating passionate sex with your partner. Such antics have been shown to increase levels of mood-boosting serotonin, as well as DHA, a hormone which acts as a building block for estrogen and testosterone, the sex hormones that increase sexual energy. Your imagination is an amazing erotic stimulant, so use it often.

72 Get in there

Making love will be the last thing on your mind if you're suffering from low sexual energy. Interestingly, though, it appears that just getting in there can kick start your desire. See if this works for you—if you can get yourself back in the mood, regular sex will improve your physical and emotional health dramatically. It increases your heart rate and deepens your breathing, providing a powerful surge of new energy. Also, when you orgasm, your body releases endorphins, which have the natural ability to make you blissfully happy.

73 Daily dozen

Renowned as one of Casanova's favorite foods, oysters are legendary aphrodisiacs. He was reputed to eat a dozen each morning in order to maintain his sexual energy. While some people claim that a fresh oyster's resemblance to female genitalia is enough to make them swoon with desire, on a more scientific note, they are a good source of zinc, which is needed for sperm production and healthy reproductive organs. They also contain dopamine, a hormone-like substance that heightens your sexual sensation and awareness.

74 Color your feelings

Which colors sing out to your emotions? Do some make
you feel happy, excited, glowing? And can they put a spring in
your step, and a smile on your face? If you're magnetized by
green, the color of nature, take a walk in the woods, lie in the
grass, and fill your home with plants. Or, maybe it's red that grabs
you with its vibrant, energizing power. Wear a red hat, put on
bright red lipstick, pick some red roses, or eat a juicy red
strawberry. Color has profound influences that are absorbed
through your eyes and skin, so use it positively to ignite your
emotional energy.

75 Kundalini

Aside from the mystical joining of male and female forces during
lovemaking, Tantric devotees aim to unite the male and female
sexual forces within their own bodies. This is known as "raising

Kundalini." Kundalini is the fire serpent supposed to lie coiled in the base of the spine; when raised, it stimulates a vast surge of energy. So, you may find it inspiring to join a Kundalini yoga class or tantra course. Through raising Kundalini, you'll experience a completely new level of consciousness and intense sexual energy.

76 Love foods

Get your sexual pulses racing with these traditional foods of love:

Chocolate contains phenylethylamine, which is thought to be the trigger for sexual desire.

Asparagus tips were valued by the Greeks, Egyptians, and Romans as an aphrodisiac.

Ginger is said to warm the blood and inspire passion.

Black pepper brings spice to the bedroom as well as to food.

Figs, with their juicy, pale pink flesh, relate the fruit to sensuality and erotica.

77 Bull at the gate

Awaken your senses and stimulate your sexual energy with ginseng and saffron. Ginseng has been used for centuries to treat male sexual problems. Ancient medical texts claim that it gives men "the power of the bull." A daily dose of either three ginseng capsules or two cups of ginseng tea helps to increase a man's sexual energy by cleansing and nourishing the adrenal glands that release male hormones. Adding saffron to food might help too, as it stimulates the reproductive organs. The ancient Greeks swore by it.

78 Honey child

Legend has it that Cupid was supposed to have dipped the tips of his arrows into honey before firing them at unsuspecting lovers. And, the relationship between sex and honey doesn't stop there—both the Bible and the *Kama Sutra* associate honey with sex. Some say that the bee pollen contained in honey may be responsible for its effects, as traces of pollen are beneficial for the prostate gland. Plus, honey contains two dozen sugars, vitamins, and minerals that give blood sugar levels and energy an instant boost. So, go on...dip your finger in the honey pot!

79 Come hither

Use aromatherapy to help assist your flow of sexual energy. The following oils have a pheromone effect that attracts members of the opposite sex.

Angelica has estrogen-like properties and is useful for stimulating menopausal or pre-menstrual women.

Cardamom is sweet and warming—it has a strong erotic effect.

Geranium is exotic, spicy, and floral, and liberates the senses.

Jasmine is a sweet, floral sedative oil with hormonal action.

Patchouli is musky, earthy, and penetrating—an excellent choice for someone who feels out of touch with the body.

Vetiver has a smoky, earthy, lemon aroma. It was used to anoint brides in ancient India.

80 Be playful

When was the last time you wrote your partner a love note, left a provocative message on his or her voicemail, shared a bubble bath, or fed him or her strawberries dipped in champagne? Creative play can be both tantalizing and stimulating, and will ignite not only your partner's sexual energy, but yours also. When you're feeling mischievous, your sexual chemistry is much more likely to flow. So, get your blood pumping in all the right directions by setting the mood with a day of play.

CHAPTER FIVE

instant lift off

81 Get the giggles

Laughter is one of the greatest tonics available. There's a scientific reason for this—laughing out loud triggers a surge of feel-good chemicals in your body, and a rush of energy that reduces levels of fatigue and tension. It also shuts down the production of stress hormones, boosts the immune system, and protects the heart. What's more, just hearing other people laugh can also invigorate your mind, body, and soul. That's why it's so great to drop in on a comedy show, or get together with a group of friends and watch a funny movie. What are you waiting for? Have a good laugh and make yourself feel great.

82 Thrills and spills

If you want an exciting surge of energy, seek out a fast adrenaline rush. Maybe it'll come from diving into an icy pool of water, standing up and talking in public, taking a ride on a roller coaster, or daring to try something that scares you out of your wits. Whatever you choose, through increased blood pressure and a faster and shallower breathing mechanism, adrenaline causes oxygen to be pumped rapidly into your system, speeding up your reactions and thinking processes. This creates immediate stimulation and an instant energy boost.

83 Brush up

The energizing effects of dry skin brushing have been known for thousands of years. By moving a soft, natural bristle brush in upward strokes over your skin, you can stimulate your lymphatic system and energize your entire body. To pep up your energy levels, first brush your lower body, heading toward the inside of your thighs. Then brush your upper body, heading toward your armpits. If you don't own a suitable body brush, you can easily improvize by using a rough-textured towel.

84 Clear the clutter

An untidy living space will quickly depress your energy levels; so, if your home has become cluttered and chaotic, take a deep breath, get to work, and throw out all those unread magazines and other junk. It only takes a few minutes to create an orderly, peaceful zone, and you'll be amazed how much more refreshed and revitalized you feel. While you're in the mood, throw open the windows and let in some fresh air, to circulate renewed energy around your room. As an extra bonus, you could plug in a small indoor water feature, to generate even more positive energy throughout your home.

85 Get out more

Look outside—is the sun shining? If it is, then step out for five minutes and enjoy the delightful sensation of the sun on your body. Without sunlight, no life would exist on earth; you're part of this immense, living picture, and the impact of sunshine reminds you of that fact. When you feel sunlight on your skin, you instinctively feel energized by the sun's powerful life force. Its warmth on your face is one of the basic pleasures of life and will lift you up in seconds.

86 Do nothing

When was the last time you did absolutely nothing? This means not speaking, reading, watching TV—not even thinking. Life is full of so many distractions, you probably can't remember the last time you completely switched off. Yet, it's more than likely that all these activities leave you feeling thoroughly exhausted and depleted. Try sitting still and being totally in the present for a few moments; don't think about what you need to add to your shopping list or what you must do tomorrow. It's not easy to switch off, but once you've figured out how to do it, you'll feel completely revived.

87 Touch force

The power of touch can quickly change the way you feel. Some forms of massage calm and relax you, others invigorate and energize. Most forms of massage work on the lymphatic system, to release stagnation. This is energizing in itself, but certain aromatherapy massages, Chinese massage therapy, Swedish massage, and Japanese therapies such as Shiatsu deliver even more invigorating effects. You can learn some basic Shiatsu techniques with a friend, and exchange a quick five-minute massage, sharing the instant energy boost of touch.

88 The vision thing

Eliminate stress before it gets out of control and destroys your energy levels. All you need do is learn how to take brief, but regular, visualization journeys. Get yourself comfortable, concentrate on your breathing to help you relax, then let yourself go completely. Think of a scenario that evokes a deep sense of serenity. It may be a remote, deserted beach with a single palm tree blowing in the breeze or a graceful swan floating on a lake. Observe the scene steadily and feel the calm throughout your entire being. Regular sessions will bring your mind into a relaxed state, ready to take on the day with new vitality and vigor.

89 Nuts about energy

When you're overworked, exhausted, or involved in challenging tasks such as long-distance driving or coping with a hangover, a handful of nuts is a fast, energy-boosting antidote. Take Brazil nuts, for example; they're full of healthy fats, are rich in selenium, and help to balance your blood sugar levels almost immediately. Or, you could munch on sesame or sunflower seeds—they're both rich in vitamins and minerals, and provide valuable Omega-6 fatty acids. Whichever you choose, nuts or seeds, you'll be rewarded with a super energy boost.

90 Flowing water

When you're completely tired out, find some moving water. If you live close to the sea, or have a river, waterfall, or stream nearby, head in that direction. Otherwise, look for a fountain in your local park or shopping mall. You may have already noticed that a special kind of energy is awakened in the presence of moving water. There's a sound reason for this; water that is in motion releases a mass of negative ions, and that's what makes you feel so revitalized and full of well-being. So, wherever you find water in motion, go there and breathe in gulps of instant, pure energy.

91 Carbo power

If you're planning to run a lot or want to begin circuit training, you're going to need every energy reserve in your body. Your muscles can only store so much expendable energy at any one time, and the rest will need to come from food. For an instant energy boost, opt for carbohydrates. Eat or drink a quick carbohydrate-rich snack such as wholemeal bread with a banana, a jacket potato with cheese, or a fruit smoothie with fresh fruit puree. That should see you striding out with renewed vitality.

92 Choose life

You may have noticed how much better you feel when you have
lots of fresh flowers and pots of growing plants in your house. It's
part of the same joy you get from seeing trees in blossom and
plants coming into bud. Contact with healthy, growing plants
makes your spirits soar and reminds you of your connection with
the entire cycle of natural life. This boost in spirits affects your
energy levels, too—when you surround yourself with living
things, there's a positive shift in your magnetic energy.

93 Energy spot

One very quick way of stimulating your body's energy is by using acupressure. The idea is that you use the lines of energy called meridians that are situated throughout your body. You can activate these at certain key points. One of the easiest points to access is on your hand. Locate the point between your thumb and forefinger on one hand, then pinch it firmly with two fingertips of your other hand. Increase the pressure gradually, hold for about one minute, then release slowly.

94 Ear massage

Have you noticed how dogs and cats adore having their ears fondled? And that some people instinctively touch their earlobes when under pressure? There's a very good reason for this; the ear is the site of important energy points that can be stimulated with acupuncture and acupressure techniques. In fact, you don't need any particular expertise to get an energy boost by massaging your ear. All you do is hold your earlobes with your finger and thumb, and, moving all around each ear, massage thoroughly right to the top. Your ears will positively tingle with pleasure, and you'll feel a rush of happy energy.

95 Energy essentials

Essential oils can be powerful invigorators when you're feeling lethargic. For a rapid energy boost, try the following:

- Massage tired areas of your body with thyme and rosemary.

- Put a few drops of either cedarwood or grapefruit, orange, and peppermint on a tissue and sniff.
- Try burning a combination of rosemary, cardomon, and ginger essential oils.
- Put a couple of drops of neroli essential oil on a shower mitt, and rub yourself briskly in the bath or shower.

96 Power shower

Stand in the shower and turn the water from hot to cold in rapid succession and for increasingly longer periods. Alternatively, lie in a hot bath for two to three minutes and follow up with a cold shower lasting 20 to 30 seconds. In time, you need to build up to a one-minute burst of cold water. Always remember to begin with hot water and end with cold. This is known as contrast hydrotherapy; its effects are said to revitalize the skin, improve circulation, and enhance energy.

97 Go barefoot

Take off your socks and shoes, and take a thrilling walk on dewy wet grass. You'll feel instantly invigorated by this unusual sensation. Moreover, thanks to the reflexology points on the soles of your feet, all the organs in your body will be stimulated. You can get a similar effect from walking barefoot by the seashore, on firm, wet sand. We're so used to wearing socks and shoes every day, we miss out on this fundamental contact; so walk barefoot from time to time, and treat your feet to an instant boost from the direct link with the earth's vital energy.

98 Take a nap

After a busy time when your body and mind are completely overloaded, you need to rest. Recording the brain's activity during sleep has shown some interesting results. When you first fall asleep, your mind goes into a resting phase, and the benefits of this can be gained by a quick catnap. Alternatively, you could try a brief relaxation technique. Shut your eyes, breathe deeply, and envision every fiber of your body in a relaxed state. Either will give you the instant energy boost you're after.

99 Power breathing

You have to breathe, every second of every living moment. Yet, how often do you think about it? Probably not at all. In fact, the way you breathe can either make you feel tired all the time or bring you to a level of energy you barely knew existed. You don't have to go to the gym to learn how to breathe properly. It takes just five minutes to energize yourself fully: breathe in and out deeply, filling and emptying your lungs fully each time. Then, pant, in quick succession for 30 seconds—let your belly expand and contract with every breath. Result? An instant high.

100 Strip off

Your body is so accustomed to being enveloped in clothing, its natural energy can become inhibited and blocked. By walking about with no clothes, you will get a simple, childlike sense of pleasure from just being in your skin. You may find that your breathing is easier, and this enhances your metabolism and stimulates your body's natural energy reserves. Ideally, you should do this outdoors—perhaps on a naturist beach. Otherwise, you can retreat to the privacy of your own home, make sure the room temperature is comfortable, close the drapes, and just enjoy being yourself.

acknowledgments

Cover photograph © Konrad Wothe/Imagestate